# 'VERUSCHKA'

## Trans-figurations

Vera Lehndorff

Holger Trülzsch

With an introduction by

Susan Sontag

205 illustrations, 163 in colour

Thames and Hudson

Printed and bound in Japan by Dai Nippon

# 'VERUSCHKA'
## Trans-figurations

# Contents

# Fragments of an Aesthetic of Melancholy

What melancholy objects these images are!

**1**  Because, first of all, they are a compendium of desires — contrasting, contradictory; impacted, immobilizing.

The desire to become fully visible, to be seen (at last) as one is; to be honest; to be unmasked.

The desire to hide, to be camouflaged. To be elsewhere. Other. The desire to impersonate someone else, but that is not other enough. The desire to escape from a merely human appearance: to be an animal, not a person, an object (stone? wood? metal? cloth?), not a person; to be done with personhood.

The desire to be emblematic. Impervious to age and the distress of flesh.

The desire to accede to the ruins of time, to be reconciled with the depredations of time; to *become* a ruin.

The desire to punish the self. The desire to place no aim before that of gratifying it.

The desire to dissolve the self into the world; the desire to reduce the world to matter, something one can inscribe oneself on, sink into, be saturated with. . . . The desire to compete with one's own image, to become image; artifact; art; form. . . .

The desire to be stripped down; to be naked; to be concealed; to disappear; to be only one's skin, to mortify the skin; to petrify the body; to become fixed; to become dematerialized, a ghost; to become matter only, inorganic matter; to stop; to die.

**2**  Because, second, of the self-conscious density of their artistic strategies and psychological impulses. Discourse and counter-discourse — like movement and counter-movement in a baroque painting.

Images about images: it is impossible not to regard these images as the ironic negation and extension of earlier ones — the de-creation of "Veruschka," the persona invented in the 1960s by a young German art student named Vera von Lehndorff, who became the decade's most celebrated fashion model. Their iconography of self-effacement is, literally, spectacular. Veruschka disappears into another celebrity image; into stones, plants; into a door, a window, a wall — "My only interest is in fusing into a background," she declares. The project of eliminating the self documented in these images is exemplified not just in their subject — a self impersonating another, a disappearing self — but in the fact that they are a full-scale collaboration rather than the work of a single artist. "No heroic ego comes through in our pictures," says Holger Trülzsch, a painter and sculptor as well as a photographer, with a large body of non-collaborative work. But their joint labors, that of one artist who is unseen (the photographer) and another artist who is straining toward invisibility (the subject), hardly lay to rest the question of ego. The self-abnegation, to the point of self-punishment, depicted here is also an affirmation of a self. For this is a space no one (only things, props) can share; there's nobody else in these pictures. They are a celebration of one person, as much as they are a record of (the staging of) that person's disappearance. Even ex-Veruschka is still Veruschka.

Although their collaboration could have taken the form of theatre or film, it seems appropriate that it take (mainly) the form of still photography, with photography limited to the role of presenting a staged — painted, constructed — reality. No shortcuts are allowed. Many of the effects of the photographs could have been achieved by certain darkroom manipulations — most obviously, by double exposure or superimposition. (As in a remarkably close prototype for some of this imagery, done in 1946 by Frederick Sommer, of a naked Max Ernst co-substantial with the surface of a dilapidated plaster wall.) Instead, the arduous way is chosen: painting Veruschka instead. What is on display is the illusionistic capacities (and more artisanal, even archaic, integrity) of painting, and this precludes manipulating the photographic medium to produce illusion. Photography, straight photography, proves the equally convincing and even more powerful creator of illusion, showing the exact equivalence, once cast in photographic form, of real clothes and clothes painted on skin, of a real wall and a person painted as a wall. The trick is to paint these well enough. Each camera exposure presupposes a long, complex, expert action, a mise-en-scène: the fabrication of an intricate artifice, then straightforwardly, truthfully registered.

Because they are "about" artifice — but with full ambivalence (is the aesthetic of melancholy always a double discourse?): both a revolt against artifice and an exploitation of artifice.

Although fashion is always the opposite of the natural, the made-up name, persona, look that constituted "Veruschka" the model was a particularly self-aware construction. And her subsequent metamorphoses have been further enactments, a hyperbolic consummation, of the idea of artifice. For instance, images from the early 1970s called Mimicry-Dress-Art invoke the artificial in two senses. The hyper-artifice of clothes or costumes painted on the body mocks the normal artifice of clothes. The hyper-artifice of the iconic traits of other period celebrities inscribed on herself mocks the icon Veruschka was in the 1960s, not just through fashion photographs but through a legendary movie appearance (as herself, in Antonioni's Blow-Up).

While Mimicry-Dress-Art is pure construction, of background (minimal) and of person, the more interesting pictures mix a high degree of artifice with a scrupulous leaving of everything as-it-is — suggesting the mixed affections of Surrealism for the found object, the lucky accident, as well as for the outrageously theatrical and artificial. (The affiliation of Lehndorff's and Trülzsch's imagery with Surrealism is a complex and reflective one.) In these pictures the full Surrealistic practice is apportioned in the following way. The background or environment remains an *objet trouvé*, not to be tampered with. The artifice is the insertion of a person. Thus a portion of a wall in the abandoned Fish Market in Hamburg (the Oxydation series of 1978) is scrupulously left as it is, and Veruschka dressed (i.e. painted) to conform to it. To *become* it.

Fashion photography itself is characteristically theatrical, the construction of tableaux that presuppose an action, a vivacious action, caught in mid-course. The particular action which these photographs depict, a metamorphosis, is represented as already achieved, terminated; indeed, immutable. What these images describe is a metamorphosis, but what they show is a stasis. They are truly tableaux: the record of an immobility. An image of Veruschka as a stone statue overgrown with moss, seated on a chair in a forest, recalls the giant statue of Neptune in the Park of Monsters at Bomarzo (near Viterbo). The work that nature and time have done there, covering the lower half of the semi-recumbent body of the god with a frayed green blanket of moss, Lehndorff and Trülzsch accomplish with make-up. But while the point of artifice in fashion photography is to halt time, that is, aging, here artifice speeds up time — to create a monster.

4 Because they are not so much beautiful as "about" the beautiful. And, consequently, very much concerned with the testing of beauty — through artifice, through distortion.

The earlier artifice, that of the fashion model, was to simulate an ideal form of oneself — to enhance an already existing, very high order of natural beauty. Here the artifice is to simulate what is *not* the beautiful woman. Another person. Or found backgrounds that are leprous, decayed, overgrown.

Ex-Veruschka — this Veruschka — is not trying to look beautiful; on the contrary. And if to create an image of beauty according to the canons of the unnatural characteristic of fashion requires an elaborate preparation, make-up, "poses," so to create these images, which inscribe something else on or encumber beauty, requires far greater feats of ingenuity, patience, and endurance. Veruschka's body and face are covered with a kind of paste onto which paint is applied. (Trülzsch describes the method as an adaptation of fresco technique.) The person disappears but beauty does not disappear (any more than does Veruschka's iconic status). It remains embedded in the image, like a more or less invisible ghost. What these images illustrate is an indomitable career of beauty — though made ugly, *still* remaining beautiful — as well as an escape from beauty. Necessarily the escape that Veruschka makes from her own beauty is staged, and, once again, for a camera. "Ex-Model Found in Wall," as the witty title of a perceptive article by Gary Indiana last year in *Artforum* has it. These are portraits of a flight, but we know where to find her: in an art magazine, or a gallery, or a book.

Ex-model still found in photograph.

5 Because, also, they are an art of excess, violence. Or morbidity. *Oxydation*, Lehndorff and Trülzsch's most memorable series, pushes furthest the depiction of a painful exaggeration: a woman naked, vulnerable, disfigured, encrusted with alien objects. (Trülzsch speaks of the "horror" of these images.) Even in the Mimicry-Dress-Art, which may seem indeed to be purely satiric, even friendly (imitating film idols, Lehndorff notes, "can only be funny or, in most cases, ridiculous") there is something gruesome; it is not just that it is clear such painting must entail a host of unpleasant, even painful, sensations. The very virtuosity of the painting, its uncanny verisimilitude, suggests something indelible — as if, should one try to remove these clothes, one could not; that one would have to flay oneself to take them off, as with the lethal wedding present Medea sends to Jason's new bride, a poisoned garment which, when the bride tries to rip it off, takes her skin with it. If to paint clothes on a naked body suggests a flaying, painting a wall on it suggests an entombment.

Because, above all, they are a mimicry of death. Becoming another person is to die to oneself, as much as becoming a thing such as a plant or a stone. Metamorphosis is not just transcendence, or mere transfiguration. Metamorphosis is also suicide — as it is for the nymph Daphne fleeing the embraces of Apollo, who, as the amorous god catches up with her, turns herself into a tree. Bernini's sculpture, in the Villa Borghese, which shows Daphne beginning to undergo her metamorphosis — buttocks, feet, calves, hands have just started burgeoning leaves, bark — is one of the most unbearable images I know.

Because they are dedicated to exhibiting the body, even as they are preeminently records of an ascesis: Veruschka's refined body straining against, merged with, coarse surfaces, filthy objects. Gaps in the body to match the opening in a door evoke a mutilation; a length of pipe stuffed in the mouth, or a metal bar pressed across the chest to provide continuity with the objects found on a wall, suggest a torture. But this body distorted, violated — like the prisoner in Kafka's "In the Penal Colony," whose punishment is having his body turned into a text — eerily registers no pain.

The body — which is all that is left of the self — becomes a mask: a screen; a barbaric pattern. Although when specifically evoking African body-painting, Veruschka is shown as standing out against a backdrop of nature, the more usual strategy of these images is to de-create the body by blending it into a background. But even this hypermaterializing (body-clothes, body-wall, body-window, body-door) amounts to a primitivizing of the self. It is also a kind of visual sci-fi, recalling Ballard's notions of the tormented body, the body dedicated to self-mutilation, in *Crash*; of the transfigured body, the body merging into the non-human, in *The Unlimited Dream Company*.

This is the opposite of pornography, which also reduces the person to a body. Nakedness (as distinct from nudity) always makes the body vulnerable. But these images isolate the body, making it solitary, pensive, beyond desire. And even though naked, the body is postulated as having no gender; it is the figure of a body: the body as support or framework or screen or surface for inscription or encumberment. In this sense, the body has no sex. Painted, Veruschka's naked body can signify the opposite sex: the image of Veruschka as a man in a pinstriped suit — even though, in this image as in all the others, we see her breasts or the pubic bush covering the female genitals. These show through the paint, like a subaqueous outline. In another sense, being naked, it is irrefutably sexual.

One characteristic topos of the Surrealistic tradition in photography is to depict the body — typically, a woman's body — transformed into an exotic object, distorted, inscribed with a visual pattern, hidden by materials. When the pattern is a rigidly geometrical one, such as a grid, it may be taken as an enactment of repression. When the patterning is layered, irregular, textured, it enacts a mode of voluptuousness. And, not surprisingly, the most sensual images often are the work of a couple: male photographer or director and woman subject (Man Ray and Lee Miller, Joseph von Sternberg and Marlene Dietrich) . . . a "labor of love" (words that Trülzsch uses to describe the painting of Veruschka's body) designed to make the woman even more beautiful; that is, present her as an object of fantasy, even more an icon of the desirable, because masked, hidden. (Sternberg's *The Devil is a Woman* is perhaps the most delirious example of this style of homage.) Lehndorff and Trülzsch's images have a far more devious relation to beauty — and one which, in effect, de-eroticizes. Though they too make the beautiful woman into "something else," put visual barriers between her and the onlooker, it is not to render her more desirable. Rather, it is to create a state in which desire is inconceivable, because the barriers are inscribed on her flesh. These are palpable, even thick, striations, not just the supple patterns of light from drawn blinds that fall on Lee Miller's naked body in Man Ray's celebrated photograph of 1931.

As in all imagery close to Surrealism, their work reposes on some hoary stereotypes about women. For such work, could one imagine a woman invisible behind the camera and a man in front, trying to disappear in the image? Not easily. Symbiotically as Lehndorff and Trülzsch collaborate, they are still doing a variation on the classic roles. Lehndorff prefers to regard herself as a self-invention: she invented herself as an object in the 1960s when she became Veruschka. Therefore, she argues, she can't be exploited, an object in the conventionally gendered sense ("... it has been I myself using myself as an object and I have therefore never felt that I was being used by others"). This is not a convincing argument. Mere intention, which is a matter of autobiography ("I have always used my self and my body as an instrument to express my ideas"), does not furnish control over what an image may project. However undoubtedly knowing and sophisticated about art and participatory Lehndorff is in the process, this alone would not guarantee that she is not functioning as an object. Still, Lehndorff is right, though more for another reason. She is objectified, literally. But she is, in these images, anything but a (sexual) object. Indeed it is precisely because of the total literalness of her objectification that she isn't an object. And this is, in some way, their point.

The fashion model is preeminently a visual object. Which means a perfect photographer's subject, as in the appearance Veruschka made in Antonioni's film. The creation of the fashion image was disclosed as the appropriation of a compliant body by the insatiable camera — a funny and embarrassing operation with the photographer writhing in a parody of sexual movements above Veruschka's body, as she assumes one pose after another on the floor.

At the end of Blow-Up the photographer is surprised to come across her at a London party; "I thought you were in Paris," he says. "I am in Paris," she replies. Always being an object might tend logically to produce its opposite, an equally exaggerated statement of the self's sovereignty: that one is always being oneself — where one is.

7 Because they are (or mime) a complex spiritual exercise.

To be only oneself, alone, carrying the whole world inside one's head; or to be only an image, something inside the world's head — these seem like opposites. In fact, they intersect in the characteristic yearnings enacted in these images.

They are detached, contemplative. Depicting a yielding to the environment, letting go, being correctly passive. (As in: "I thought you were in Paris." "I am in Paris.") But they are also saturated with the will.

What Lehndorff and Trülzsch are engaged in are acts of prowess, of daring, of excess. Their aim is to perform new feats of fooling the eye. Not only images about images but images in competition with images: setting the barre higher and higher. In one sense, they are about faking. In another sense, they are rigorously truthful images — fully paid for.

And what if we were to discover that they were after all done by superimposition or double exposure? Surely our view of them would change. It is in fact the rejection of facility, the acceptance of ordeal in order to create these images, that gives them their meaning. Thereby they make a point quite opposed to that famous photograph Yves Klein had taken of himself in 1960, "The Painter of Space Casts Himself into the Void," which shows Klein, having just hurled himself from the mansard roof of a house in a Paris suburb, diving upward. Finding out that photograph was a photomontage, we are hardly surprised, for we knew it wasn't a picture of Klein's suicide ... and we never really believed he could fly. But neither is the photograph discredited in any but a perfunctory sense, for it was never more than a solo image, a one-time description of the self, and therefore a stunt — one which simply turns out to be a visual rather than a physical stunt. Lehndorff and Trülzsch's pictures have another status. They document not a single gesture but an ongoing project, or yearning — for transfiguration, which *means* redescription. The project of redescription has to be an open-ended series. Not a stunt. Therefore, it is crucial that it be a physical as well as a visual re-description of the self.

But it, too, mimics a suicide.

8   Because they show a purely material way of being in the world. Which is not in contradiction with their preoccupation with form, their wish to *be* form.

"I am only a form, the shape of a human female body, with no personal gesture or expression, merging into a second form . . ." But this is an extravagantly pas-sionate avowal.

The argument of these images is not unlike that of romantic opera, which re-quires the (female) voice to give itself up to a measured excess, thereby pro-ducing the felt necessity, the rightness, of the death of the character sung by the diva. But instead of seeking a maximum expressiveness, as voices in opera do, what is sought here, and associated with death, is a maximum inexpressiveness. And in contrast to the excess favored in opera, which is produced by a yearning for another person, for that person's love, this is a monodrama: narcissism at the stage of martyrdom.

In the throes of her expressive death — which is what martyrdom is — Ver-uschka behaves much like any Saint Sebastian, whose face simply doesn't reg-ister what is happening to the body. It is part of the standard iconography of Christianity that the expression and demeanor of the martyrs be strikingly at odds with their graphically depicted, atrocious experience, as if they were obli-vious to what the body is undergoing; they can express serenity, even joy. For this martyrdom, there is just impassivity.

9   Because they make something so vivid, seductive, out of the conquest of eros (a beautiful woman) by thanatos (thinghood, the non-organic). Leopardi's wonder-ful conceit, a dialogue between fashion and death, here becomes incarnate. Per-sonality is erased through becoming matter, but this negative territory is not a void; it also harbors the propensity to bourgeon. Decay is not only dissolution but a mode of rampant proliferation.

These are images which illustrate that unspeakable instinct, the opposite of libido, in the service of which Veruschka continues to dis-identify herself, to display her un-erotic status. She is effectually dead, empty, not present. Yet she is not lifeless. Rather, she is imprisoned, or lurking, or hiding. Such strong energy for un-being is a richly resonant paradox. (Including the paradoxes of solipsism masquerading as, aspiring to, spiritual detachment.) The desire to un-be pro-vides a new, ardent relation to the world. The old Fish Market in Hamburg, the warehouse storing huge bales of old clothes in Prato where Lehndorff and Trülzsch plan to work next — the whole world becomes a stage for dis-appearance.

10   Because they take time's ruins as a premise for invention, for allegorizing.

The predilection of Lehndorff and Trülzsch for decaying surfaces, rotting architecture is a mode of lament. To finish with impersonation, whose purpose is ridicule, and concentrate on the contemplative mimicry of impersonal environ-ments — fusing into a background which is often one "in a state of decay and is related to our culture," Lehndorff notes summarily — has brought a steady growth of solemnity, gravity, power in their work. Satire wanes, as they incorporate the much-remarked pathos of large commercial and industrial spaces of the early modern era: an abandoned hall or warehouse or factory fallen into desuetude. It is a taste at least as well-developed in France as in Germany — the opposite of, and complement to, the florid rational spaces of Ledoux, photographed extensively by Trülzsch on his own, not long ago; he now lives in France part of each year. These are our sites of melancholy, our imaginary prisons. (And work marvellously when used, left virtually as is, for theatrical or exhibition spaces: the burnt-out Bouffes du Nord in Paris, the Entrepôt Lainé in Bordeaux.)

To be exploited as muted cultural commentary does not exhaust the eloquence of ruins. As an allegory of personal as well as historical loss which cannot be repaired, they are an old figure in the aesthetic of melancholy. They are also a recurrent feature of nineteenth-century sentimental narrative, as Philip Fisher has pointed out, in which the work of art is the solemn memorial to the ruin, which is itself the inverse of a monument. But in a sentimental narrative or image there is always a plurality of personages. No one is ever truly alone, or wants to be. (Indeed, characters are usually defined principally as members of a family.) Sentimental art requires the presence of a witness, for whom the stories of woe or images of desolation provide a training in pure feeling, a sharpening of feeling. What characterizes the aesthetic of melancholy is that there is no witness, only a single, unmoving protagonist — one who does not witness desolation but *is* desolation — and whose complete identification with the desolate scene precludes feeling (its exemplary form: tears), whose gaze is unresponsive, withdrawn.

Because, therefore, they depict an exacerbated pensiveness.

In the standard image of melancholy, the self is depicted as marooned, solitary, motionless, overwhelmed, becalmed. Melancholy since late medieval poetry and visual imagery has been "Dame Merencolye" or "Tristesse," a lean pale woman wrapped in poor or ragged garments. In the most famous image of all, Dürer's, she is a bulky figure, heavily clad; she sits leaning head onto left hand, staring morosely; her right hand, holding a compass, is in her lap. One of the more inventive aspects of the imagery proposed by Lehndorff and Trülzsch is that Melencolia prefers to stand rather than to sit, has shed her clothes — she turns out to be a great beauty — and is not looking out or down but is simply, calmly absent: her eyes are usually closed.

One sees the immobility, the heaviness. One forgets the willfulness and doggedness of melancholy. Its currents of reckless energy. Its propensity to ardor.

One sees the pensiveness; one forgets the thought. Perhaps even Dürer's Melencolia is just waiting for someone to express surprise that she's here, that she isn't in Paris, so that she too can reply, "I *am* in Paris."

SUSAN SONTAG

March 1986

1

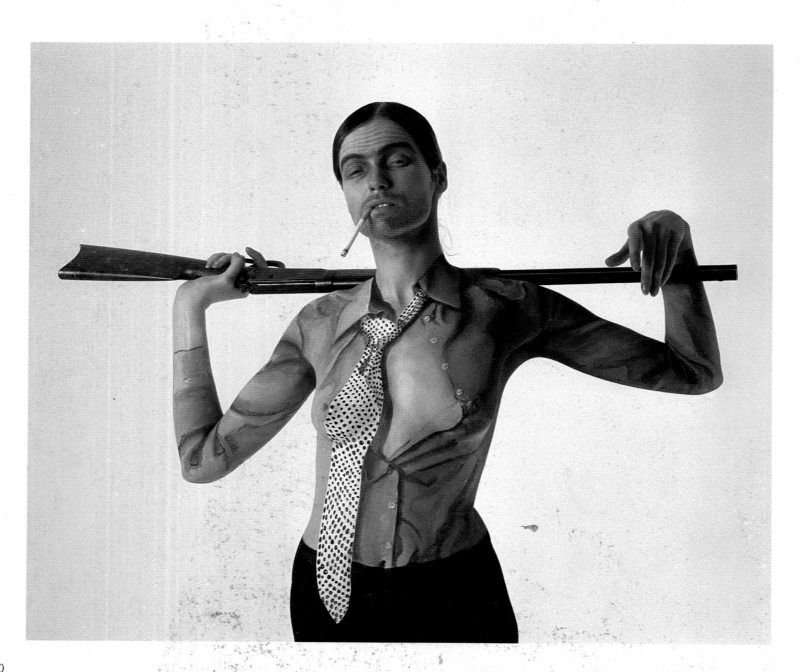

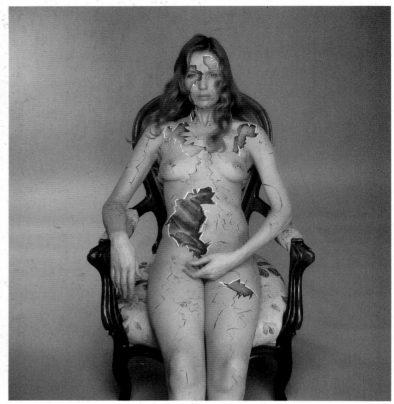

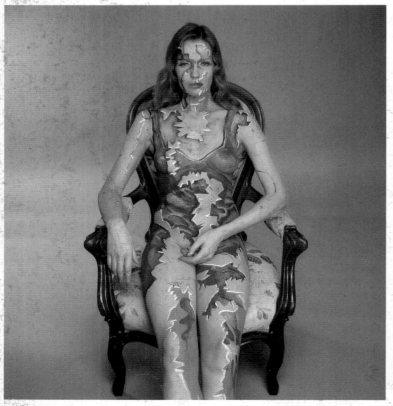

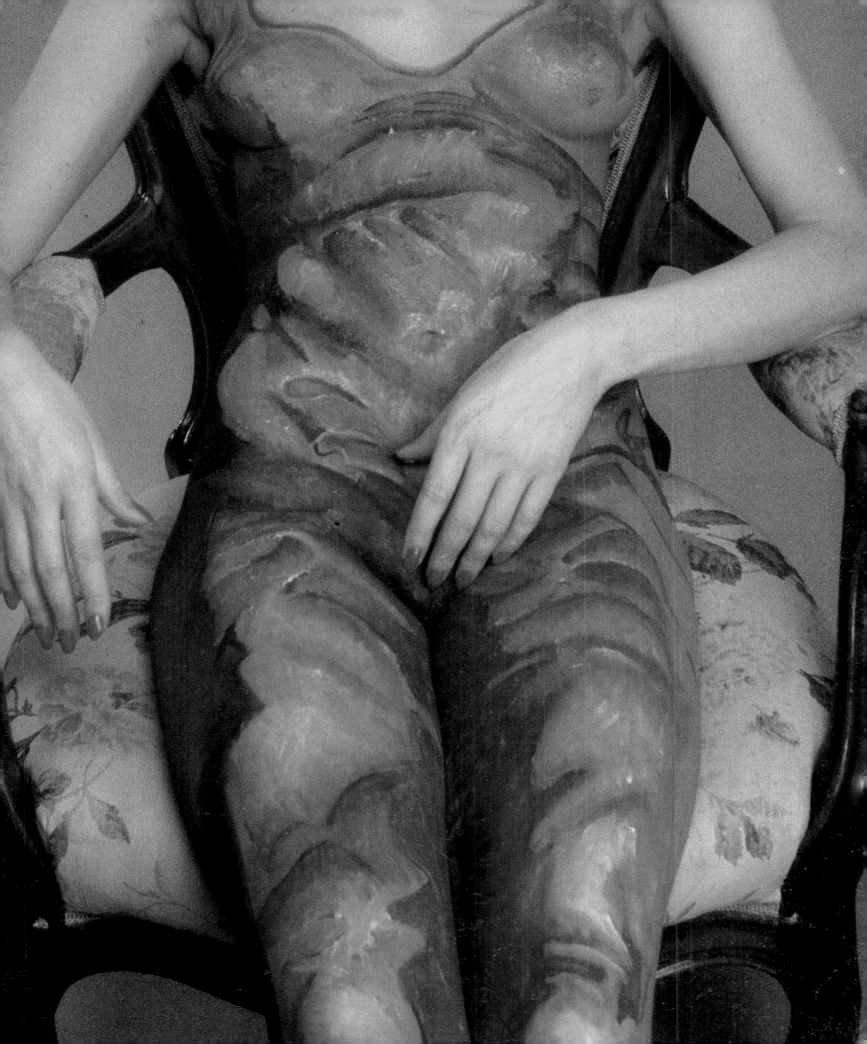

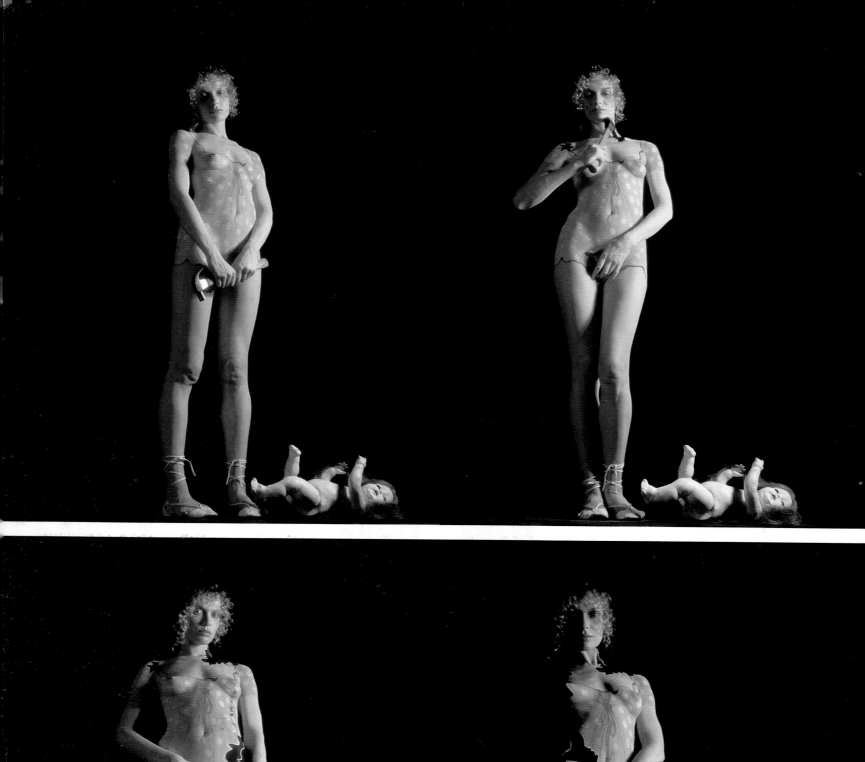
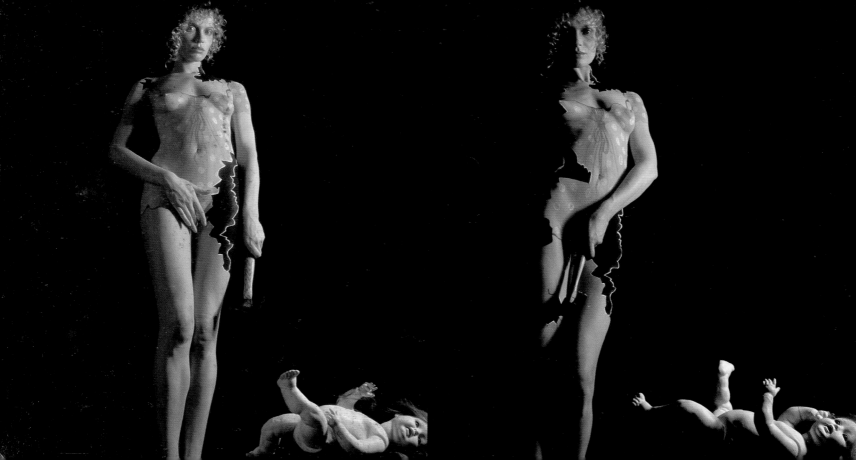

2

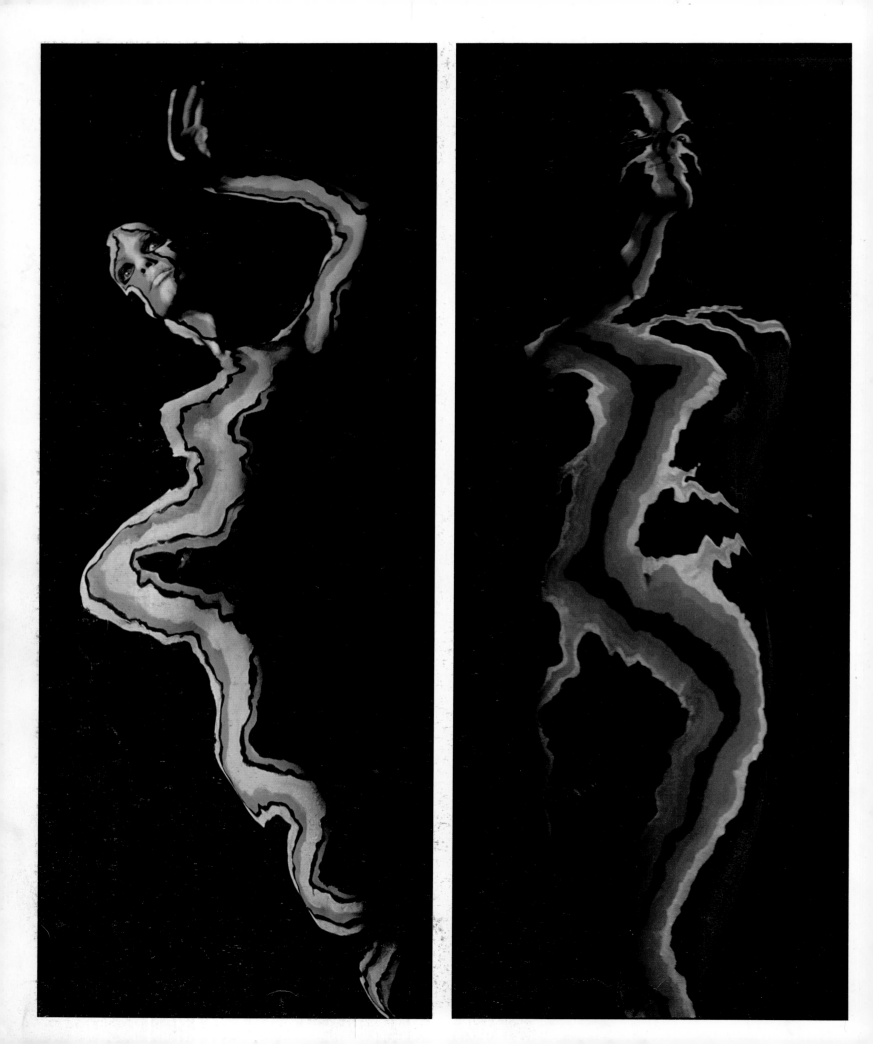

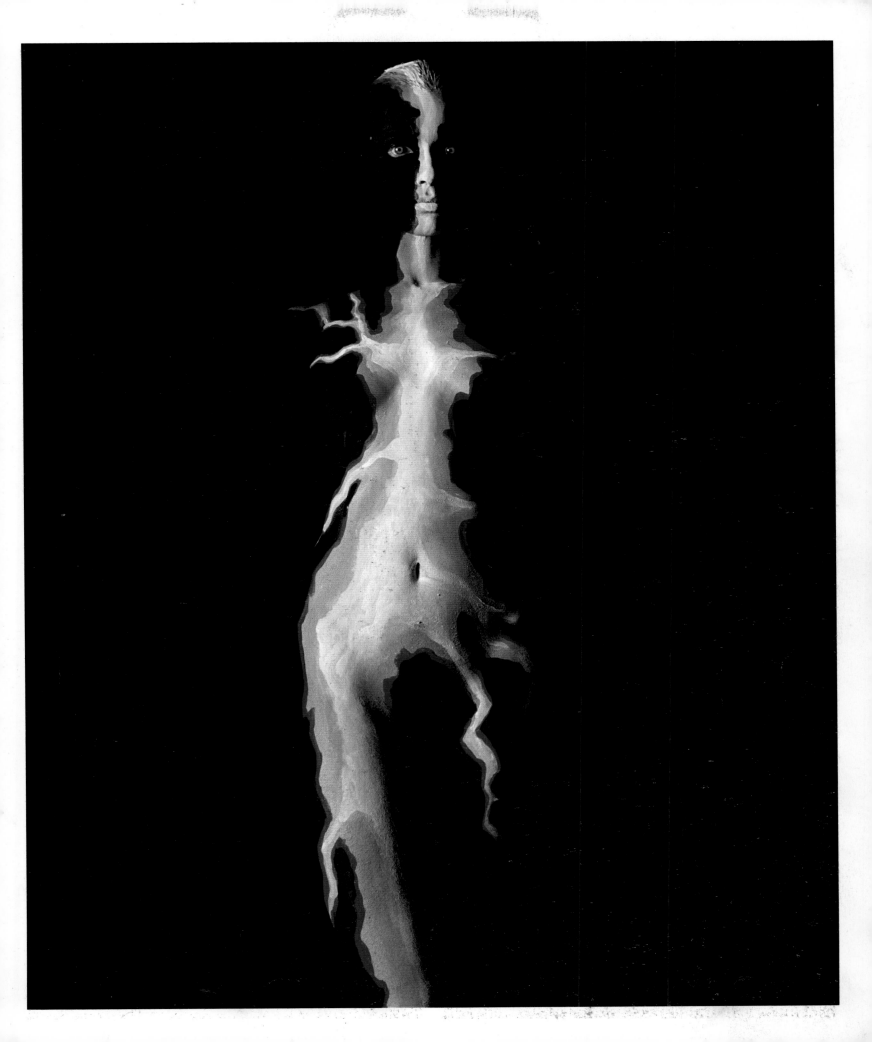

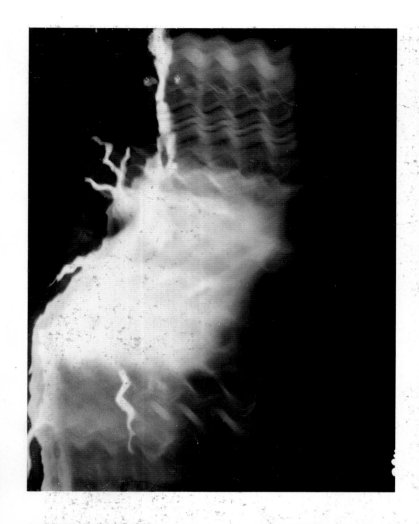
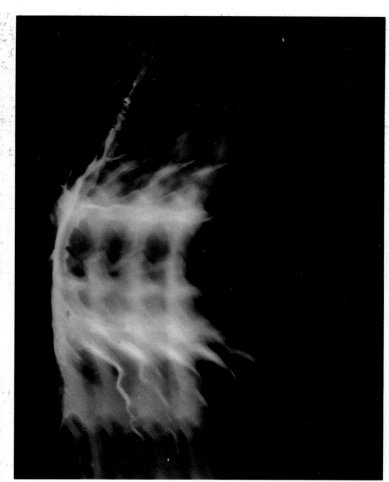
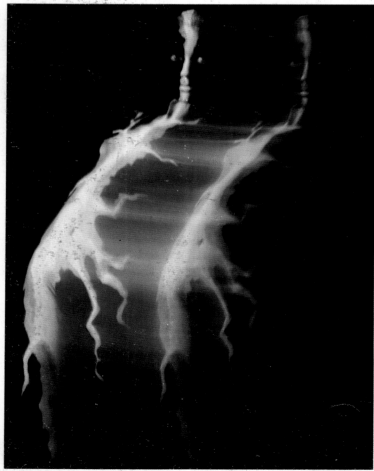

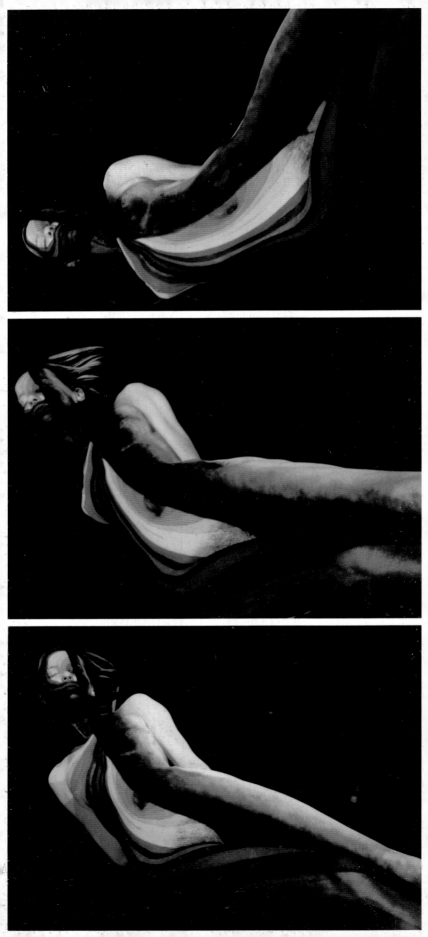

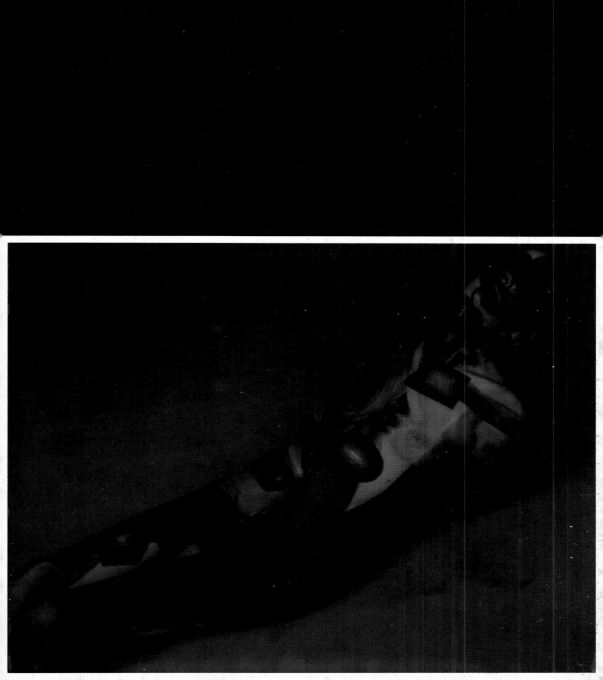

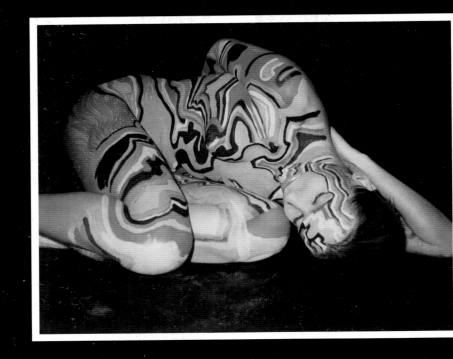

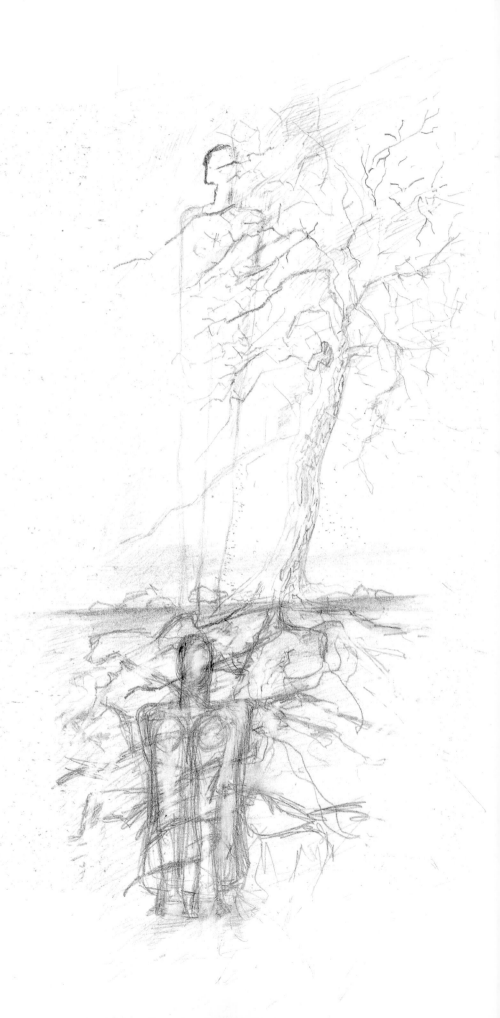

3

4

Oxydographie, Fenster, Akt, 1925                    Peter Thelen, Vogtländorff

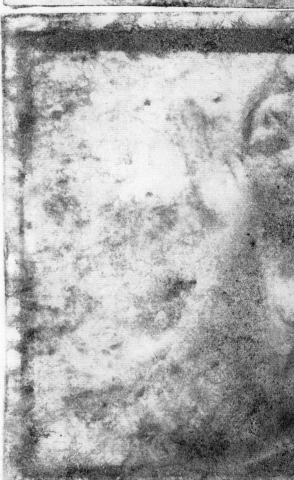

5

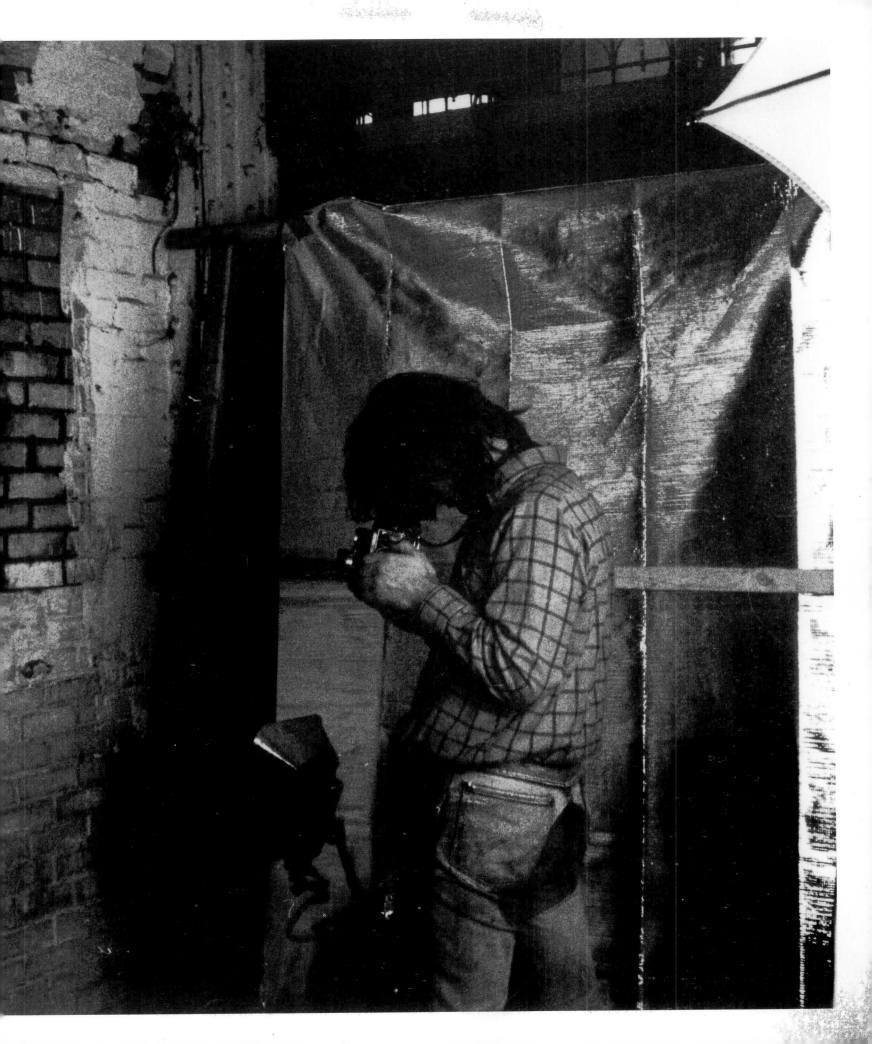

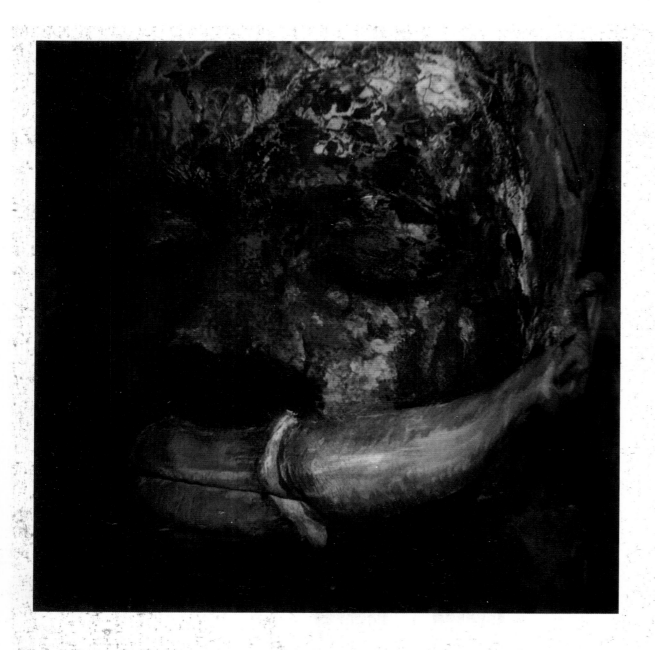

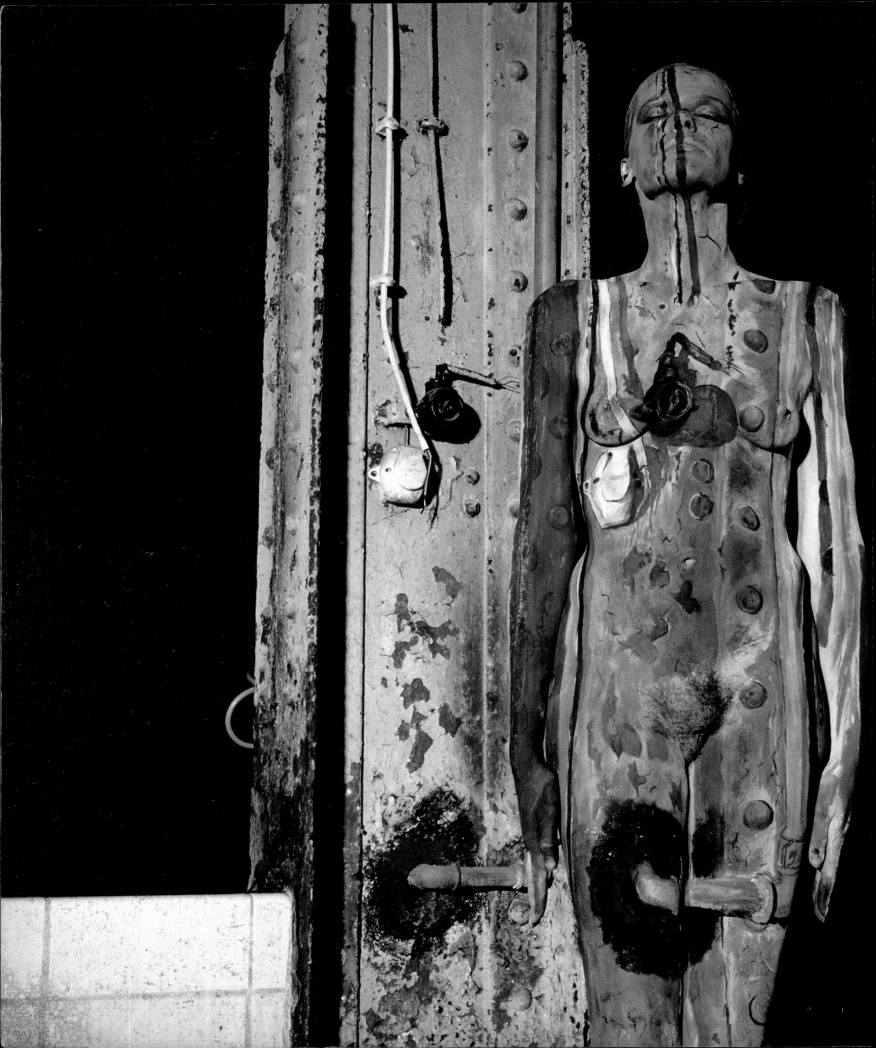

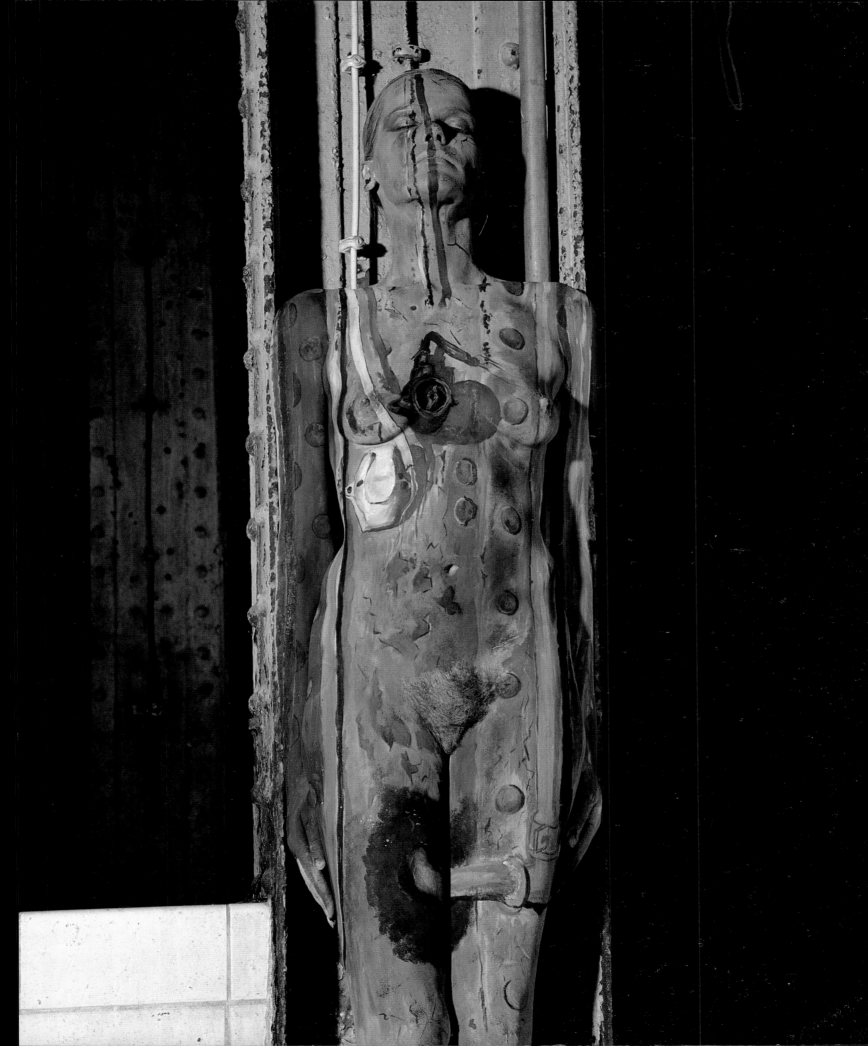

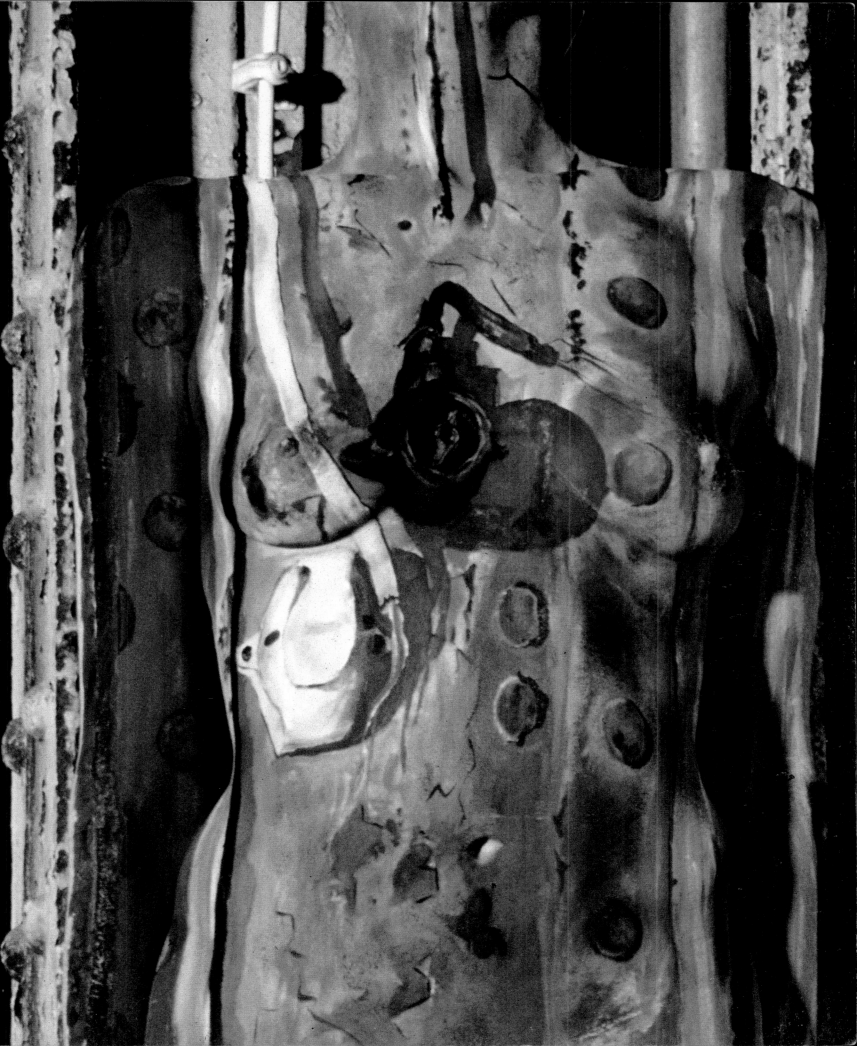

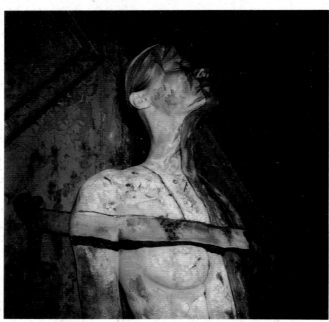

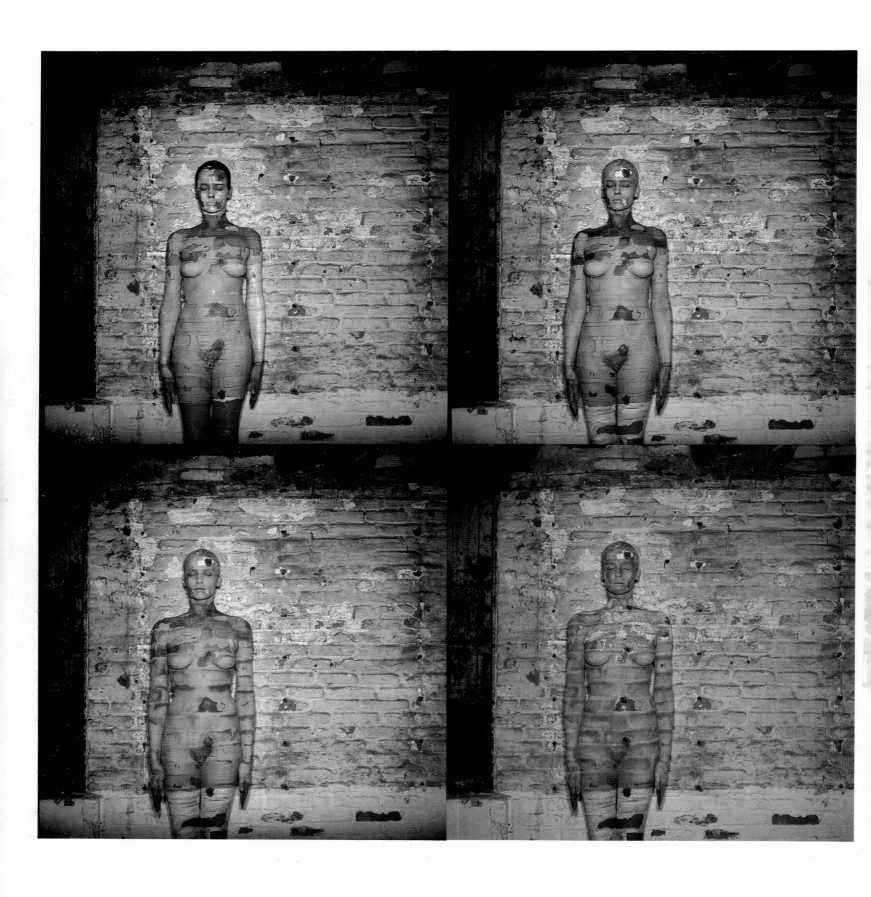

Oxydographie Hamburg 1979

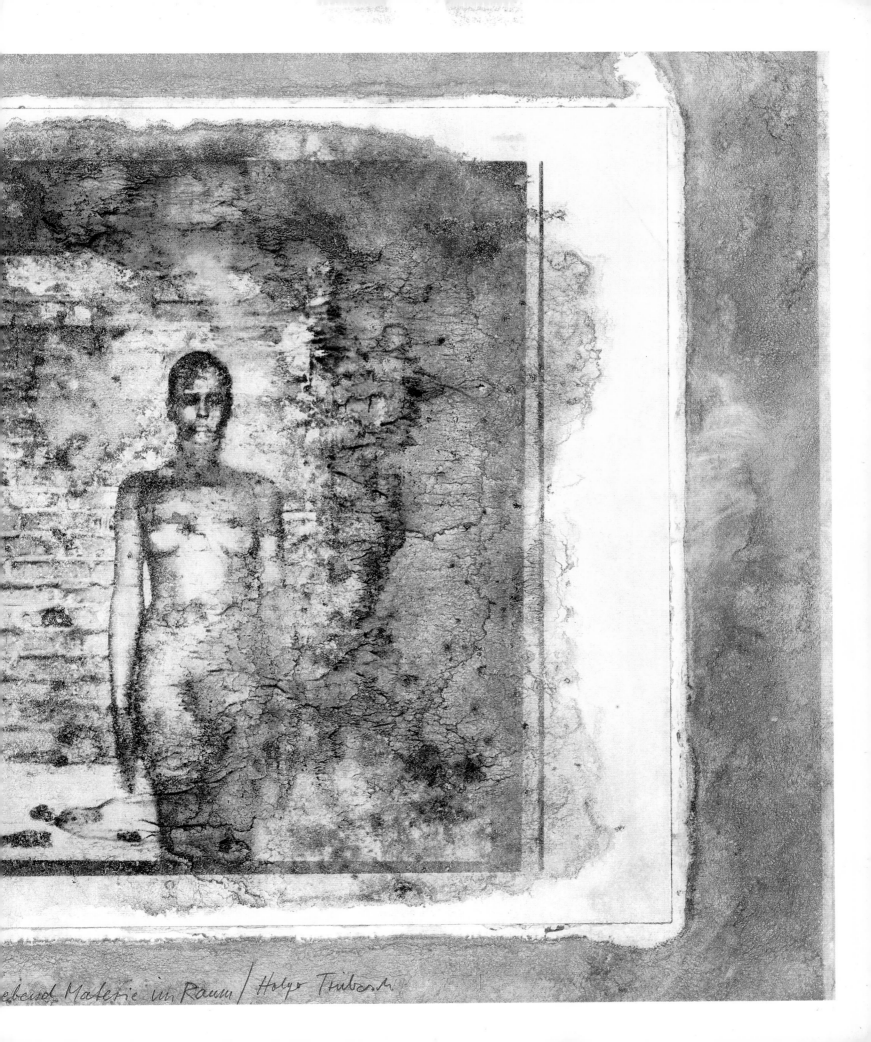

ebend Materie im Raum / Helge Thilbad

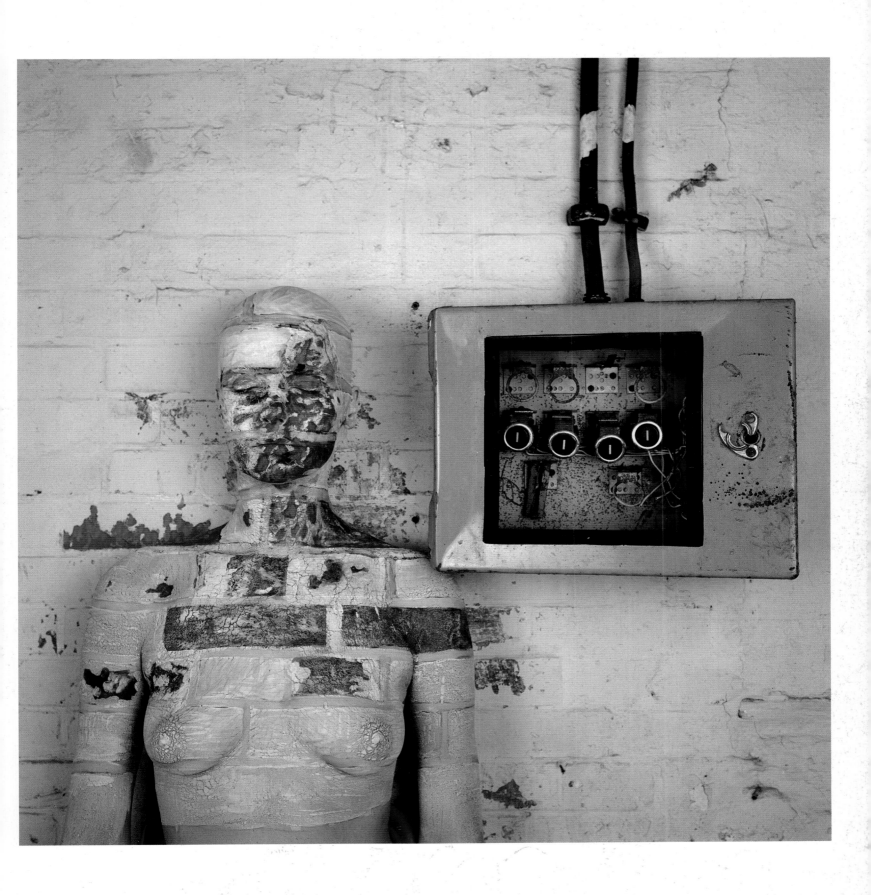

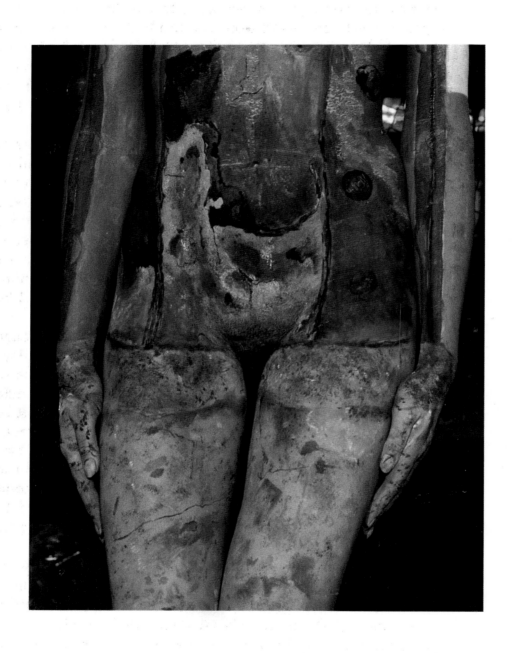

# Fusing into the Background     VERA LEHNDORFF

When I was studying painting, I was sometimes disturbed by the thought that one day I would have to have a job like everyone else, and the idea of commercializing my paintings was very alien to me. At first I thought I could use my experience with colours to work as a textile designer, but after a short period of study I realized how depressing this was: everything had to be flat, patterns had to repeat themselves endlessly and after a lot of work you ended up with a marketable curtain or some synthetic fabric that would be made into an ugly dress. And I said to myself: Was it for this I spent two years studying colour and composition?

I was reminded, when I was painting, of the frustration and sadness I had felt as a child at the unbridgeable distance between myself and other people, and myself and objects. I had wanted to be able to merge with whatever I found beautiful – usually things in nature or things for which I felt an affinity. I can remember embracing a tree in the hope that I myself would change into one. When I was six I sat outside day after day to watch the sunset, enjoying its light, and I thought: If I run to the hills behind which the sun has disappeared, I should be able to catch up with it and dissolve into that orange sphere. I tried this many times until at last I realized it was not possible. I learned that there was distance between all things.

In the 1960s, when I was working as a fashion model, I thought it would make a more interesting photograph if I changed the colour of my skin, giving the image a strangeness that would distract attention from the often very boring dresses. As a model I could transform myself into many different characters. Soon I began to paint myself as different animals and plants, knowing that they are often more beautiful than we are. The nakedness of human skin always disturbed me. By painting myself I could create the illusion of having feathers, fur, scales or leaves. When I saw a photograph of myself painted like that, it pleased me. Camouflaging myself also made me feel that the public could not trap me so easily. The photographs could reveal something new both to myself and to others. I don't think I could have done modelling for so long were it not for the enjoyment I derived from such transformations.

When I started to paint on myself, the colour and I were one: there was no 'between'. My work was now consistent with my conviction that there had to be a coherence between things: the object and the created picture, me and the picture, me and the object, my experience and the picture, my experience and the object, the viewer and the picture, between me and the viewer, the experience of the viewer and the object and the picture. This experience of coherence between us and the world around us is one of well-being; it produces a sense of affinity with whatever it is with which we come into contact. I have always used my self and my body as an instrument to express my ideas, but it has been I myself using myself as an object and I have therefore never felt that I was being used by others. So if people perceive me as an object I feel that is not my problem.

At the end of the 1960s, I thought of painting my head like the stones of a terrace where I had been sitting one afternoon. Later I did the first stone head surrounded by stones. When I met Holger, at the beginning of the 1970s, he thought this was the start of something interesting. Our work is like a silent performance in which two persons are involved: Holger and myself. There are no spectators. When we met, Holger was a musician; before, he had painted and sculpted; on meeting me he became interested in photography. We began to work a lot together, living in the country, in Germany. It was a little bit like playing: whatever came into our minds, whatever I felt I wanted to become, we did.

We started doing the first wall, door and window pieces, and perspective began to enter the work. We were now both painting on my body. A little later we did the dress paintings (*Mimicry*), ironic poses and attitudes of men and women in show business. The dresses were painted by Holger alone. Unlike the work in which I become part of the background, in which I try to identify with an object, the dress paintings aim to show that when we try to give up our own identity and take over somebody else's personality (that of a film idol, for instance), it does not work; it can only be funny or, in most cases, ridiculous. By painting the dresses on the body we avoided simple imitation and transformed the body into an artificial object that demonstrates a typology of poses related to ways of dressing, and so provides an ironic commentary about our time, its idols and its clichés.

I have a great admiration for so-called primitive body painting. Of course we cannot understand the significance it has for those who practice it; the colours and signs they use on their bodies are narratives and have a meaning that remains closed to us; we can perceive it only as an art form, related to their own cultures and lives. It would be pointless to try to imitate it. We did once attempt something in Africa, not anything that was meant to bear any relation to African body painting, but a work called *Signs and Animals*. In it a white woman simply tries not to fade away in the tremendously strong African landscape by using strong colours and forms painted on her skin.

Body paintings, unlike conventional paintings, cannot be done every day. For one thing, it is physically not possible; for another, it is not interesting to do it over and over again unless a new idea emerges, like coming across some place that evokes thoughts about appearing and disappearing. My only interest is in fusing into a background. The place is often one which is in a state of decay and is related to our culture. *Oxydation*, for instance, is done in this spirit.

Sometimes people wonder why I should want to identify myself with doors, windows or walls – all this matter that is either dead or in the process of decaying. They think that maybe Holger and I are trying to create in our work a narrative about me. This is not so. As far as we are concerned, I am only a form – the shape of a human female body, with no personal gesture or expression – merging into a second form: a window, a door, a wall, etc. For me, things around us have symbolic meanings: a door is not only a door, it could also be an entrance or exit into something different and new; windows are also eyes through which we perceive and therefore communicate with the outside world; walls can be seen as separations, disconnections or forms of protection. I feel that it is important to deal with the surface of things because the surface may reveal to us a secret world, a new aspect. I believe strongly in the multiplicity of aspects in an image or a situation, in things seen from many different viewpoints, in resisting habit – the passive acceptance of how through convention we see ourselves or others. An artist's vision has to do, after all, with new ways of seeing, ways which make the artist and the work one and the same thing.

# The Real and the Illusory     HOLGER TRÜLZSCH

'What is characteristic of the language of art is the profound identity between the structure of what is signified and the structure of the sign.'

. . . there is one phenomenon that is just as important as writing, and that is photography.' (Claude Lévi-Strauss, *Entretiens avec* CL-S, 1959)

We too have heard the 'voice of Surrealism' (André Breton, 'First Surrealist Manifesto', 1924). However, our work has nothing to do either with the 'catalytic role' (*ibid.*) of the *objet trouvé* or with the surrender to the laws of the unconscious that takes place, for example, in the use of 'automatism' in writing and painting. Nor does 'objective chance' (*ibid.*) play an essential part; nor does the paradox of the 'Readymade'. But who is not affected by Surrealism – in particular by the crude violence of the derivative 'surrealistic' images on LP sleeves, posters, book-covers, etc., images that make our day-to-day life ever more colourful, fresh and cheerful – whether they spring from business acumen or from artistic impotence.

Nor do we have anything to do with 'Symbolism', which in all its artistic manifestations put far too much emphasis on the mysterious.

The painting of Vera's body is a touch, a labour of love; it is also, simultaneously, the elimination of that body so that it no longer belongs to her and is no longer identical with her. The human body inserts itself into the picture as an outline without a self. Seen without its illusionistic (anamorphic) perspective, the body emancipates itself from its own materiality and becomes an autonomous pictorial and sculptural unit. Fragmented, the body distorts its component parts into 'abstract' curves traced on its own convex surface. In order to find a formal counterpart for this transformation we have – as its logical sequel – adopted ever more expressive postures until the transformation came to match our conception in the context of the picture as a whole. Expression, to us, signifies a gentle, subtle shift of posture, the features of a face without a gaze. It is not the iris of the eye that smiles but the lines of the face around the eye, creating a familiar, endless multitude of expressive nuances. A face whose features have been obliterated is outside this whole culture of expressive communication. The crude materiality of flesh yields no familiar human signals. Only by a supreme effort can I suppress the sheer horror that grips me at the sight of this expressionless 'countenance' and its nameless mass. Only the eye still reveals the vanished person behind it, the person who speaks to me and to whom I speak. What is unendurable to me is that with the elimination of the face my own ego can no longer be reflected in it.

Through painting Vera's body I can rid myself of the expressive ego of the painter and disappear behind my work; no heroic ego comes through in our pictures. We have succeeded in leaving behind the self-perpetuating painterly gesture of the Post-Post-Modernists, whose relentlessly self-surpassing pursuit of Individualization has long since reduced them *ad absurdum*. We have nothing in common with the 'pseudo-painting' movements, amateurs who can see nothing beyond their own daily productions, ruled by the idea of novelty, and who mark the progress of their own tedious decline through the constant repetition of ingeniously twisted imitations: an 'academicism of signs' – as Claude Lévi-Strauss called it in a radio interview in 1959 – that allows no meaning to emerge.

Our work embodies the rules of a technique of representation that we find in Hans Holbein, and of a technique of painting akin to that of fresco (in which the surface is coated with an admixture of lime). The colour fully reveals itself only when dry. As in the 'coating' technique of fresco, the painting on the body must be kept moist to stop it flaking off. We have to know and judge the effect of the colour as it is applied. The colour value of the support, the surface on which the painting is done – the skin – plays an essential part here; its degree of redness changes as a result of overheating (over a period of eight to fifteen hours) and influences the overall tone of the painting.

The end product, as in the lithographic technique, is transferred to paper in multiple colour layers through absorption by a coat of gelatine, in the dye-transfer technique that we use. We do not overpaint the photograph, nor do we manipulate the technical process of photography by projection, double exposure, etc.

Painting and photography are interlinked in our work as a consequence of their specific characteristics, which we employ consciously as a means to art: painting creates the anamorphic illusion that the 'Vera' body sinks into the structure of the real background; and at the same time photography transforms 'reality' so that it appears as it is, a perceptual phenomenon based on illusion.

Both processes result from the interference that is set up between the perception of the 'real' in an artificially created illusion and the perception of the 'illusory', which in its photographic reduplication takes on the perceptual quality of the 'real'. The opposites displace each other and undermine the habitual process by which we take in what is called a depiction.

This interchangeability and interlinking of cognitive processes serves to synthesize the artistic space in which we carry our 'hallucinatory manipulation – wherein one does with bodies *as one wants*, so that gradually they fill every compartment of desire'.

The Sarrasinean artist tries to undress appearance, tries always to get *beyond, behind*, according to the idealistic principle which identifies secrecy with truth: one must thus go *into* the model, *beneath* the statue, *behind* the canvas . . . *behind* the paper . . . (though what is behind the paper is not reality, the referent, but the Reference, the 'subtle immensity of writings'). (Roland Barthes, S-Z, chapter 54, from transl. by Richard Miller, Hill and Wang, 1974)

Each time we have to re-encode the body with the outline, form and colour of a new background – masonry, plaster, wiring, power-points, iron components, or whatever – it is necessary to give prior thought to the site to be used and its precise 'painterly' and 'formal' potential in relation to the body and the space, before the body is fragmented and reassembled.

I think our works should be classified as painting, in accordance with Kandinsky's theoretical precept that real materials should be adopted as aesthetic elements and that painters should paint with everything. But because we regard 'reality' as an aesthetic form in itself, interlinked with our painting and entirely equal to it in status, we therefore abolish the distinction between reality and painting – and reality *becomes* painting.

*Translated by David Britt*

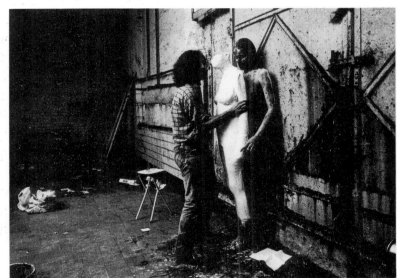

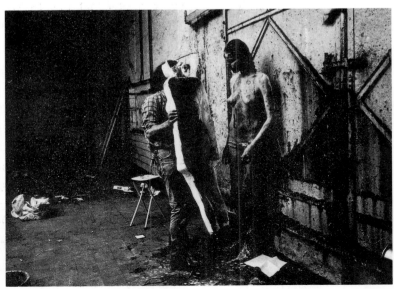

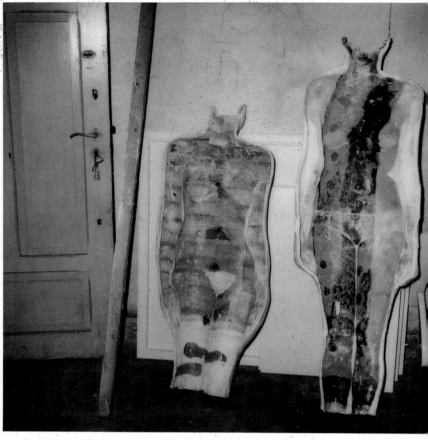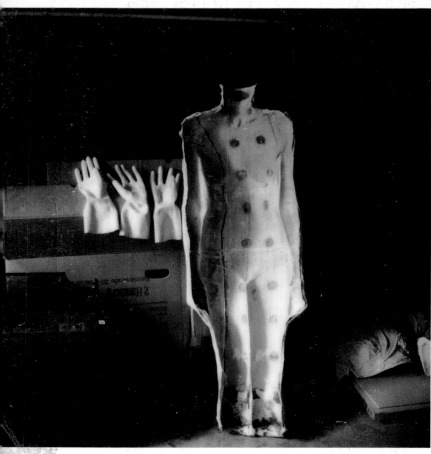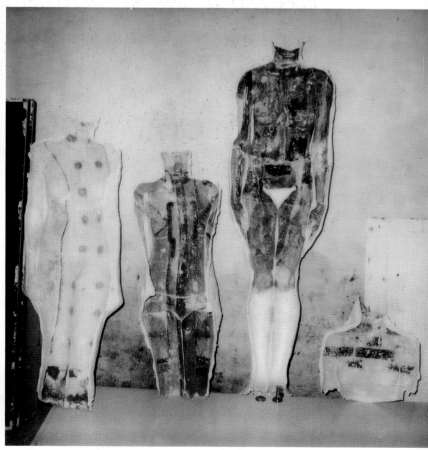

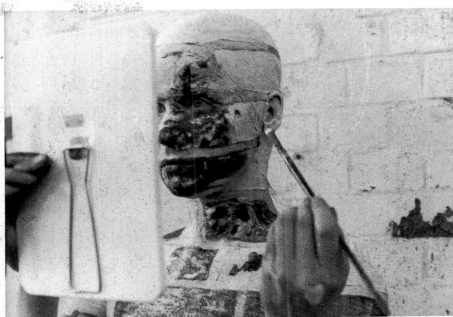

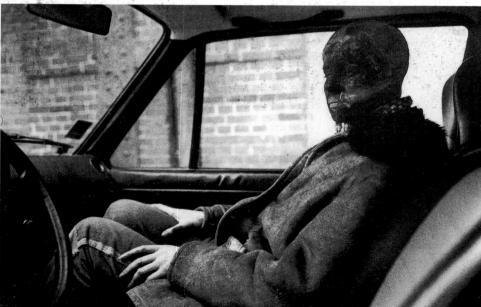

# List of illustrations

56  Stone head, Rome 1969 (photographed by Rubartelli)

57  Wall with snow, Peterskirchen 1970. Cibachrome, 35 x 50 cm (13¾ x 19¾ in), edition of 6

58  Forest-piece at Schnaitsee, Performance II. Cibachrome, 105 x 105 cm (41⅜ x 41⅜ in), edition of 6

59-61  Hörzing Grotto, Performance 1971. 3 images. Cibachrome, each 105 x 105 cm (41⅜ x 41⅜ in), edition of 6

62-63  Three stone heads, Peterskirchen 1971. Cibachrome, each 24 x 30 cm (9½ x 11⅞ in), edition of 10

### Peterskirchen, Spetse, Paros

65  Faded wall, Peterskirchen 1971. Dye transfer, 40.5 x 26.5 cm (16 x 10½ in), edition of 25

66-67  Stable door, oxydized sheet metal, Peterskirchen 1975. Triptych. Dye transfer, each 30.5 x 29.5 cm (12 x 11¾ in), edition of 10

68  Stable window, Peterskirchen 1975. Cibachrome, 49.5 x 49.5 cm (19½ x 19½ in), edition of 10

69  Holger Trülzsch, Oxydographie 1975, Stable Window. Pencil, chalk, silver bromide on paper, 30 x 40 cm (11⅞ x 15¾ in)

70  Details of 71

71  Wooden door with window, Peterskirchen 1975. Cibachrome, 49.5 x 49.5 cm (19½ x 19½ in), edition of 10

72  Inner door, Peterskirchen 1976

73  Inner door, Peterskirchen 1976. Dye transfer, 30 x 30 cm (11⅞ x 11⅞ in), edition of 35

74  Green window frames, Spetse 1975. Dye transfer, 30.5 x 29.2 cm (12 x 11½ in), edition of 75

75  Black door to the garden, Peterskirchen 1975. Dye transfer, 30.5 x 29.5 cm (12 x 11⅝ in), edition of 75

76-77  Blue sky and wall, Spetse 1975. Cibachrome, 105 x 210 cm (41⅜ x 82¾ in), edition of 6

78  Face covered/uncovered, Performance, Spetse 1975. Cibachrome, 30 x 40 cm (11⅞ x 15¾ in), edition of 6

79  Holger Trülzsch, Oxydographie 1975, Face covered/uncovered. Pencil, chalk, silver bromide on paper, 30 x 40 cm (11⅞ x 15¾ in)

80  Open front door, Paros 1977. Dye transfer, 27 x 41.3 cm (10⅞ x 16¼ in), edition of 75

81  Detail of 80

82  Detail of 80, with open eyes. Negative print

83  Closed front door, Paros 1977. Cibachrome, 40 x 60 cm (15¾ x 23⅝ in), edition of 6

84  Window door, Paros 1977. Dye transfer, 27 x 41.3 cm (10⅝ x 16¼ in), edition of 15

### Oxydation (Hamburg-Altona 1978)

86-87  Installation of bodysculptures in the old Fish Market: 'Archaeology of a Temporary Oxydation', Hamburg-Altona 1978

88  Installation pipe head. Living bodysculpture. Polaroid, 8 x 8 cm (3⅛ x 3⅛ in)

89  Installation of pipe driven through head. Dye transfer, 40.5 x 40 cm (16 x 15¾ in), edition of 29

90-91  Iron beam with socket and light switch. Diptych. Dye transfer, each 40.5 x 40 cm (16 x 15¾ in), edition of 29

92  Iron beam with socket, light switch and unpainted face. Living bodysculpture. Polaroid, 8 x 8 cm (3⅛ x 3⅛ in)

93  Detail of 91

94  Vera Lehndorff 1978, untitled. Gouache, chinese ink, pencil on paper, 21 x 13.5 cm (8¼ x 5¼ in)

95  Brick wall. Living bodysculpture. Polaroid, 8 x 8 cm (3⅛ x 3⅛ in)

96  Crumbling wall sitting. Living bodysculpture. Polaroid, 8 x 8 cm (3⅛ x 3⅛ in)

97  Iron beam with water pipe and electrical cable. Dye transfer, 40.5 x 40 cm (16 x 15¾ in), edition of 29

98  Crumbled wall head. Cibachrome, 40 x 60 cm (15¾ x 23⅝ in), edition of 10

99  Iron beam head, Cibachrome, 40 x 60 cm (15¾ x 23⅝ in), edition of 10

100-101  Bolted iron door, red oxide. Diptych. Dye transfer, each 40 x 40.5 cm (15¾ x 16 in), edition of 29

102-103  Bolted iron door, red oxide head. Cibachrome, 40 x 60 cm (15¾ x 23⅝ in), edition of 10

104  Vera Lehndorff 1978, untitled. Gouache on paper, 21 x 13.5 cm (8¼ x 5¼ in)

105  Red oxide arching out. Living bodysculpture. Polaroid, 8 x 8 cm (3⅛ x 3⅛ in)

106-107  Taking possession of the old Fish Market. Tableau of 9 silver bromide-paper prints, each 30 x 40 cm (11⅞ x 15¾ in), edition of 6

108-111  Triptych. Three dye transfers, each 40 x 40.5 cm (15¾ x 16 in), edition of 29

112-113  Bricked-in iron beam, left side of triptych door, fist and legs. Cibachrome, 40 x 60 cm (15¾ x 23⅝ in), edition of 6

114-115   Bricked-in iron beam, left side of triptych door, head. Cibachrome, 40 x 60 cm (15¾ x 23⅝ in), edition of 6

116   Holger Trülzsch 1978, untitled. Pencil on paper, 42 x 40 cm (16½ x 15¾ in)

117   Living matter in space. Silverbromide paper, 30 x 40 cm (11⅞ x 15¾ in), edition of 29

118   Living matter in space. Silverbromide paper, 30 x 40 cm (11⅞ x 15¾ in), edition of 29

119   Holger Trülzsch, Oxydographie 1978. Chalk, pencil, silverbromide on paper, 30 x 40 cm (11⅞ x 15¾ in)

120   Living matter in space. Silverbromide paper, 30 x 40 cm (11⅞ x 15¾ in), edition of 29

121   Holger Trülzsch, Oxydographie 1978. Pencil, chalk, silverbromide on paper, 30 x 40 cm (11⅞ x 15¾ in)

122   Living matter in space. Silverbromide paper, 30 x 40 cm (11⅞ x 15¾ in), edition of 29

123   Brick wall head. Living bodysculpture. Polaroid, 8 x 8 cm (3⅛ x 3⅛ in)

124-125   Holger Trülzsch, Oxydographie 1978. Pencil, chalk, silverbromide on paper, 30 x 40 cm (11⅞ x 15¾ in)

126   Living matter in space, sequence of movement. Three images. Silverbromide paper, each 30 x 40 cm (11⅞ x 15¾ in)

127   Brick wall next to electrical box. Dye transfer, 40 x 40.5 cm (15¾ x 16 in), edition of 29

128   Iron door barred. Living bodysculpture I. Polaroid 8 x 8 cm (3⅛ x 3⅛ in)

129   Iron door barred to the River Elbe. Dye transfer, 40.5 x 40 cm (16 x 15¾ in), edition of 29

130   (top) Iron door barred. Living bodysculpture II. Polaroid, 8 x 8 cm (3⅛ x 3⅛ in)

(centre) Iron door barred. Living bodysculpture III. Polaroid, 8 x 8 cm (3⅛ x 3⅛ in)

(bottom) Iron door barred. Living bodysculpture IV. Polaroid, 8 x 8 cm (3⅛ x 3⅛ in)

131   Iron door barred. Living bodysculpture V. Polaroid, 8 x 8 cm (3⅛ x 3⅛ in)

132   Work in progress, crumbling wall

133   Crumbling wall. Dye transfer, 40 x 40.5 cm (15¾ x 16 in), edition of 29

134-135   Holger Trülzsch, Oxydographie 1978. Pencil, chalk, silverbromide on paper, 30 x 40 cm (11⅞ x 15¾ in)

136-137   Iron pillar with drainpipe. Diptych. Dye transfer, 40 x 40.5 cm (15¾ x 16 in), edition of 29

138   Iron pillar with drainpipe. Living bodysculpture. Polaroid, 8 x 8 cm (3⅛ x 3⅛ in)

139   Iron pillar with drainpipe head. Living bodysculpture. Cibachrome, 49.5 x 49.5 cm (19½ x 19½ in), edition of 29

140   Detail of 141

141   Part of cracked wall next to fuse box. Dye transfer, 40 x 40.5 cm (15¾ x 16 in), edition of 29

142   Vera Lehndorff 1978, untitled. Gouache, 16 x 24 cm (6¼ x 9½ in)

143   Figure in front of the Fish Market. Polaroid, 8 x 8 cm (3⅛ x 3⅛ in)

144   Detail of 112-113

## Working Images

149-151   Preparation of the casts on Vera's body. In the negative form of these bodysculptures, the color of the paint will be preserved. We are building them for an installation in the Fish Market

152-153   Plastic tent over wooden construction. While we are working in our action-space protected from the cold, the space of the hall and its construction is always visible. Its aesthetical appearance is fragmented by the wooden construction of the tent, its different angles and perspectives, which create an aesthetical total where we both dominate the hall and are at the same time dominated by its field of force

154   On our way home people seem quite shocked by Vera's evil appearance, and turn their heads quickly away

155   The plastic veil is getting more and more dense, partly because of the Scotchtape pasted over it to cover the mischievously cut rents, and partly by the replacement of some of the ripped off parts with new plastic material. Day after day it is becoming a *real* "soziale Plastik"

156   Night after night our hidden audience, the bums who live in this hall, protect their rights to an undisturbed living space by smashing into pieces everything we have built up. Slowly we coalesce with the aesthetic of this place and get used to the dust, the vermin, the stench of urine and excrement